Florence Lydia Snow

The Lamp of Gold

Florence Lydia Snow

The Lamp of Gold

ISBN/EAN: 9783743312364

Manufactured in Europe, USA, Canada, Australia, Japa

Cover: Foto ©ninafisch / pixelio.de

Manufactured and distributed by brebook publishing software (www.brebook.com)

Florence Lydia Snow

The Lamp of Gold

THE LAMP OF GOLD

BY
FLORENCE·L
SNOW

CHICAGO
WAY AND
WILLIAMS

M DCCC XCVI

Copyright, 1896, by Way & Williams.

PRINTED AT THE DE VINNE PRESS.
TITLE-PAGE DESIGNED BY EDMUND H. GARRETT.

"I fancy you are mistaken," said Hilda, smiling. *"There was a meaning and a purpose in each of its seven branches, and such a candlestick cannot be lost forever."*

The Marble Faun.

CONTENTS

The Sacred Fire 11

Daybreak 27

Mid-morning 43

Noon 59

Western Windows 75

Eventide 91

The Perfect Light 107

THE SACRED FIRE

I

A poet heard, one happy summer day,
A tender maiden speaking low and sweet,
And, caring only that he might obey,
Plunged deep into the waters at her feet,
Where, in the slime of ages long since dead,
He found a lamp of tawny, twisted gold,
And, bearing it aloft above his head,
He pleaded that its story should be told.
But lo! she only turned her radiant eyes
Upon the distance where the Holy Land
Rested at peace beneath the peaceful skies,
Nor touched the treasure in his eager hand, —
  Then breathed upon him, "Who enthralls the night,
  Of his own spirit must control the light."

II

If it were but a dream he never knew
When afterwards he lived the time again;
But from that hour his highest purpose grew
To finer feeling for the needs of men.
The virgin metal beaten from the soul
Of God's own workman lifted out and up
On each good branch its consecrated bowl,—
And his the task to fill each wondrous cup.
For he had wandered through the wilderness,
And through the desert had been curtained in;
In many a temple he had knelt to bless
The boundless love that triumphs over sin;
  Nor would he ever spare the purest oil
    That he had pressed from out the heart of toil.

III

He read once more, as on the sacred page,
The mystic meaning of the deathless fire
That blent into the Christly heritage
In full fruition of the world's desire;
And slowly tracing through the eastern lands
The flame that burnt with such transcendent power,
The faith that blossomed for its deep demands
Burgeoned again into more perfect flower.
And every flower in turn, transformed to flame,
Illumined every heaven-lifted dome
That, bravely built upon the mighty Name,
Upheld the glory of eternal Rome, —
  Then fixed a path upon the circling seas,
  Forever leading unto wider ministries.

IV

The life that holdeth love a thing apart
From any slightest labor must disclose
The utter weakness of the rarest art
Its dearest aspiration ever knows.
Who does not give in constant sacrifice
The buoyant blood that courses through his veins
Has less than naught for all his best emprise
In righteous ruling of his utmost pains.
For without love no worthy work may be,
And without death creative power were done;
Herein there lies all happy victory,
And here all growth and gladness are begun.
  Cast in a mould beyond a fleck or flaw,
  'T is only love that can fulfill the law.

V

And even as the majesty of day
Gives to the world a part of every hue
The sun has braided in each royal ray,
So love to many a chord must e'er be true.
Surely it sifts its life and loveliness
From every turn and tint of circumstance,
Nor leaves the purity it would express
To any shadow of untoward chance;
But never wearied in its patient quest,
It searches out its own high destiny,
And by the truth made wholly manifest,
It gains the touch of perfect liberty.
  What seeming good shall ever be denied,
  The freedom of the spirit must abide.

VI

What endless lines of beauty curve about
The central force that doth all things create!
What splendid color, woven in and out,
Imbues the wonder of the earth's estate!
And, ever widening to the reverent hand,
What deep dominion lies in human skill
Exalted, step by step, to understand
Some little measure of the sovereign will!
From round to round the sweet, triumphant breath
Inspires the humblest craft and highest art;
The greatest word a mighty poet saith
Finds in the lowliest life a certain counterpart.
  So be that it is good when it be done,
  All work is beautiful, all beauty one.

VII

And thus my poet mused, his ripening thought
Reaching into the changing harmony
Whereby the changing centuries are taught
How days long done are linked with days to be.
The Voice that throbbed across the formless deep,
Setting the shining spheres in ordered space,
Must speak forever in the precious sweep
Where wandering souls are given primal place.
And with the burden of a glad new song
Upon his ready lip he went his way,
His spirit lifted all serene and strong
Unto the splendor of a vast new day.
  And whoso rightly heareth shall behold
  The light that burns within the lamp of gold.

DAYBREAK

I

When first I felt the wonder drawing near
'T was when, a helpless alien, all alone,
I bent my head beneath the dark and fear
That pressed upon me from the great unknown.
There was no thought of any light to be
In all the limits of the brooding night;
No glimmer in the dense obscurity
To give the slightest hope of surer sight.
Yet even as the motionless profound
Was moved to meet the first transcendent day,
My soul was stirred within its deadening round,
In dim desire of some superior sway,—
  And then the word spake through me from afar,
  And stayed the shadows with a silver bar.

II

And, slowly wakened to the broadening line
That slowly cleft the smothering mist in twain,
My senses came a little to define
The earth and sky in half-considered gain;
Then, with the flushing heavens bent to me,
And some strong certainty beneath my feet,
I turned my face full on the mystery, —
My poet's music sweeter and more sweet, —
For, once aware, in my great impotence,
Of rhythm and of courage, all my heart
Yearned forth beneath the mystic Where and Whence,
The How and Why that measure life and art,
  And dreamed of curious questions one by one.
  Had not the dreaming dawn for once begun?

III

O blessed wonderings of the blessed time
When life looks out upon the rose and gray
That hold the secret of a perfect prime
Folded within the promise of the day!
When life looks out, and all its ignorance
Is like all knowledge in the endless space
That may not feel the wavering touch of chance
In any realm of its unmeasured grace.
The buoyant breath of universal air
To every throbbing thought makes due reply;
And throbbing thought, in its unfretted care,
No marvel in the meaning can deny;
  And, working out the forces of new birth,
  The heights and depths reveal their matchless worth.

IV

No wonder when the dayspring from on high
Descended on the weary sons of men
The angels chanted in the kindling sky
Such joyous chorus over and again,
Since every daybreak, in some certain sense,
The splendor of that morning should unfold
In tender glimpses of omnipotence
Beyond the filmy veil of gray and gold;
And every spirit that should come to see
Its own great gift of gladness in the light
Should join the deep, encircling harmony
In freedom from the subtle bonds of night,
   And dark and dawn, forever reconciled,
   Should mirror forth the glory of the Child.

V

'T was well for me that on that precious morn
When heaven and my poet found me out,
And to myself my nobler self was born
Beyond the power of questioning or doubt,
I was a child in body as in heart,
With radiant reaches of my time to grow,
And, stretching up, absorbed my little part
Of all my little world rejoiced to show.
And yet I knew not anything was small,
For, looking through so sweet an atmosphere,
The widest portals opened at my call,
And mighty mysteries came close and clear,
  And all the royal heralds of the sun
  Brought me their boundless treasures one by one.

VI

The after years hold nothing half so sweet
As this first conscious turning toward the hills,
And first discoveries so fair and fleet
Among the shining fields of daffodils;
No after song-search may at all compare,
However fortunate the soul may be,
With this first sense that all the ambient air
Is filled with song but waiting to break free;—
When budding life breathes in on every hand,
The life and love of stone and stream and flower,
And grows, not knowing how to understand,
Into some likeness of creative power,—
  Careless of words, but reaching for the tone
  Made through the ages for its very own.

VII

In such delight and fertile eagerness,
My sovereign singer, I reached forth at length
Thy miracle within me to express,
In timid test of all my utmost strength;
But all my efforts only could repeat
The magic measures I had learned of thee, —
Could only take thy rhythm to complete
My broken thread of groping melody.
Yet, breathing over each beloved line,
And shaping every note in reverent rote,
I came, in sudden greatness, to define
The power and purpose of thy leading note;
  And then my heart leapt out free as a bird —
  I too should sing, — and, singing, should be heard!

MID-MORNING

I

He values freedom most who once hath been
Deprived of his accustomed liberty;
And when my stupid teachers shut me in,
The outer world was everything to me.
To follow round the wearisome routine
Of tedious lessons that were never done
Inspired the morning with a dazzling sheen
It only knew when lessons were begun;
The sunny sweetness of the beaten way
By which I reached betimes my prison door
Was ne'er so sweet as when its bright array
Thro' troubled texts shone brighter than before,
  And painted over every tiresome task
  The rarest pictures human heart could ask.

II

How good it was beneath the mounting morn
To loiter past the hazel thicket where
The baby nuts in such green growth were born
And hid away with such especial care!
And then to lean against the ancient elm
That always watched my journeys to and fro,
And, looking upward, find the fairy realm
That only birds and children ever know!
Or, stretched full length upon the mossy ground,
Where fringing fern so tenderly uncurled,
How dear it was to catch the elfin sound
That sometimes echoes from the under-world,
  And learn the secrets of the quiet nook
  So fondly cherished by the faithful brook!

III

Oh, sweeter far than flute or flageolet
That ever caught the breath of Arcady,
The silver stream at every turn was set
To some new phase of liquid harmony;
And when I crossed the shining stepping-stones,
The magic music, slipping slowly past,
Wove such a web of soft, enchanting tones
It could not fail to hold me safe and fast;
Nor could I fail to give back song for song
In murmurous croonings 'neath the happy spell,
Forgetting that I still must fare along
Until I heard the master's brazen bell.
  What poor exchange for wood and stream and sky,
  The utmost skill that he might hope to try!

IV

How great a puzzle that the lettered lines
Upon one page make only puzzles clear,
While through another all the sunlight shines,
And marshaled ranks of poetry appear.
But whoso follows, though with lagging feet,
The mighty music of the mighty host
In every problem finds a rhythmic beat,
And hardly knows which reading means the most.
And so I came, because my poet willed,
To see how God's two worlds together grow —
The springing fountain must be wholly filled
Before the grateful waters overflow;
  The poorest master then had learned to teach
  Some bit of beauty that I longed to reach.

V

From book to book, like some quick honey-bee
That flits all day from flower to fresher flower,
I dipped into each wondrous treasury,
And gathered sweetness with unwearied power.
The wildest weed and fairest garden-rose
Gave forth the bounty of the summer sun ;
Impassioned rhyme and cultivated prose —
All sorts of blossoming — to me were one.
And so I built from cell to golden cell,
Scarce conscious of the swarming human hive
Where countless other creatures stored as well
The same delight in everything alive.
  Is not the nectar of the dear unknown
  Most deeply generous when sipped alone ?

VI

To feel the joy of effort more and more,
To gleam and glow with iridescent thought,
In very gladness opens wide the door
Upon the selfish hoard so sweetly sought.
But none may enter in who does not share
His own attainments to the last degree, —
Such interchange hath everything to spare
And everything to keep most sacredly.
And when I found a bright prophetic face
Impressed with all I meant some time to know,
I could not hide the slightest gift or grace
That in my solitude had charmed me so, —
  No matter what ambition may bestir,
  Love is the only true interpreter.

VII

Together — O the dear, delicious word —
We pressed upon the smiling universe,
Uniting all that we had seen and heard
Like golden coin within a common purse;
Together cast a splendid horoscope,
Each for the other in our eager pride,
Nor ever dreamed the most ethereal hope
Too frail or fair to be a proper guide.
And so each forward step in our emprise
Brought such increasing wonder and acclaim,
We knew that we might lift our favored eyes
To any height that we should chance to name,
   And every marvel of the precious time
   I fashioned over into precious rhyme.

NOON

I

As when a happy mocking-bird essays
To imitate amid the forest choir
The rarest and most varied roundelays
In very overflow of glad desire,
My joyous verse attempted many a strain
In likeness of the world's great minstrelsy,
Nor counted any cost that might attain
The skill that lies in such dear mimicry.
But while the bird, despite its borrowing,
Perfects the beauty of its own sweet song,
'T was such device that taught me how to sing,
And how to listen to the gifted throng, —
  And though I tried so much without avail,
  I felt the force that cannot wholly fail.

II

How can I ever pay the debt I owe
To that high company whose royal line
Upgathers every thought that life can know
In harmony so deep and so divine?
How shall I prove me worthy of the love
That lifted me into the radiant sphere,
And placed within my hands the keys thereof
As one ordained for vision free and clear?
O love, my Love, and love of poetry,
Although thy largess hath no measurement,
There is no debt that can be due to thee
Save poetry and love in full content;
   But no one can fulfill his dearest vow
   Without the double seal upon his brow.

III

The poet's question and its sure reply
In the beginning gave my quickened touch
The strength my Love was quickest to descry,
Rejoicing that it promised me so much.
And wrapped so close in love I could not guess
Between the two great masters of my heart,
That either was the greater or the less,
Until the world began to praise my art.
Then I was certain that my verse should take
The noblest that was in me hour by hour,
And even love, for its surpassing sake,
Should sacrifice all claim upon my power,—
  Could any consecration e'er abide
  That did not thrust the inmost self aside?

IV

Who has not journeyed in the pride of youth
Amid the perils of a mountain track,
Where but a step, regardless of the truth,
Would quench all hope in some abysmal wrack?
And thus I traveled on my chosen height
Along the dreadful verge of self-deceit,
Veiled in vain-glory from the gracious light
That God had sent to guide my wayward feet.
And, hastening on, my danger unconfessed,
I trembled o'er the chasm of despair,
Until love drew me back upon its breast,
And gave me new belief and courage there.
  And loving my dear Love so much the more,
  I loved my art still better than before.

V

This love of ours was no exotic bloom,
Though all so rare in every tint and vein;
No gorgeous growth freighted with dense perfume,
Perfected through imprisoned heat and rain;
It was the flowering of the out-door air,
The common soil, and cool, caressing dew,—
The simple bounty of the heavenly care,
And fraught with heavenly odors through and through.
Its rootlets struck so deep into the mold,
That every finest fiber found the heart
Wherein the hidden springs of life unfold,
And burgeon out in endless counterpart;
  And, facing up before the searching sun,
  It touched its high commissions one by one.

VI

To give again all that it ever knows
Through earth and sky in calyx-cup and seed, —
The purpose of the humblest flower that grows
Must be the spirit of the highest creed;
And our great love in no wise could forget
How wide a service in our boundary
Demanded that its marvels should be met
For every gift with utmost ministry.
Art could be great only as love revealed
The truth triumphant and the sacred way,
And most exalted love were half-concealed
Only as art should perfectly obey.
  With such a message always to repeat
  What inflorescence were so passing sweet?

VII

As one who is anointed from on high
For every holy issue made for men,
For love and labor in untold supply,
I set me to my singing once again.
The wondrous work had fully chosen me
Beyond all question or remotest doubt,
And I could only fashion fearlessly
What life and love together pointed out.
So, like the Sibyl at her wave-washed door,
Who cast her countless leaves upon the wind,
Freely I flung abroad my gathering store
For any needful traveler to find, —
  When all the mid-day burns so crystal-pure
  The slightest utterance is strong and sure.

WESTERN WINDOWS

I

The gladdest singer voices many a strain,
Beneath the anguish sobbing through the world,
That feels the impress of the sacred gain
Within the heart of grief so purely pearled.
He cannot rightly gauge the major chords
That measure out his own great happiness,
Without the minor meaning that affords
The fullest force to all he would express.
But though he touches every precious note
His art demands for perfect harmony,
The sweetest song that pulses from his throat
Only defines the singer's sympathy, —
  He may not reach the poet's highest grace
  Till he has stood with Sorrow face to face.

II

I told myself the truth, divining how
The life about me found its finest tone
Within the beauty of the holy vow
The spirit makes through suffering alone.
To sing my joy were service far too small,
When grief demanded comfort everywhere, —
What could avail unless I too should fall
Into the deeps and learn to triumph there?
I thought my strength sufficient to endure
The keenest trial known to human heart,
Nor felt my calling could be really sure
Till pain had purged the dross from out my art, —
  But when the moment of my trial came
  Only the common weakness met the flame.

III

How could I know the swift-descending fire
Would kindle all about the golden shrine
Where I had heaped the fruits of glad desire
Withholding nothing in my rare design?
How could I see, so suddenly bereft,
The hand of mercy in the cruel loss,
Or feel that any slightest hope were left
Beneath the burden of so great a cross?
And so, forgetting Christ had gone before
Along the crowded way to Calvary,
My stricken soul but questioned more and more
How it could live through such deep agony, —
  How should the mother-heart be comforted,
  If all its highest quickening were dead?

IV

O dear Strong-Heart, how had I ever kept
The feeblest faith but for thy steadfast hold
Upon the surety I had most bewept
As thrusting me away from its fair fold?
I had not come in my distress to prove
The precious power I could not hope to reach,
When through the glass of our transcendent love
I sought so much of heavenly grace to teach.
I had but touched upon the boundless sphere
Of God's compassion, measured from our own,
Nor felt my straitened spirit draw so near
The sacred source of all that we had known;
  Oh, but for thee, this righteous chastening
  Had well destroyed the least desire to sing!

V

The fiercest storm that sweeps across the land,
Blotting the glory from the summer skies,
Unfolds new leaves of love on every hand
All richly charactered for chosen eyes.
And when the conquering sun shines forth again,
As if he were rejoicing through and through,
The endless service of the wind and rain
From breadth to breadth expands before the view;
Then heaven and earth unitedly reveal
Such wondrous depths of God's encircling care
That all the depths beyond can scarce conceal
The fuller revelation other-where;
  No longer holden, I had come to see
  What all the strain and stress had done for me.

VI

I looked abroad into the broadening west
As I had looked into the growing morn,
Eager to make the promise manifest
Enfolded in the beauty yet unborn.
Yet with the wonder of the early day
I had the touch of every passing hour,
And every messenger that came my way
Had given me some portion of his dower.
Both good and ill, but always inmost good,
Had shaped me ready for my grave new birth,
And in my grave new joy I understood
What worlds of rhythm bind us to the earth, —
  The lark that soars upon the highest round,
  Still keeps its nesting-place upon the ground.

VII

The heavenly chrism fresh upon my head,
And every power renewed in quickened trust,
I could but follow where the spirit led,
And simply sing whatever song I must.
I could but share, as in the mid-day glow,
The dearest forces throbbing to my hand;
But I had come by so much more to know
The wider issues waiting my demand, —
By so much more, that every thread of thought
My larger purpose loyally defined,
In all the shining reaches that I sought
Held me the nearer to all human kind;
   And more and more the words I found to speed
   Were drawn from out the depths of human need.

EVENTIDE

I

Why should it be when one has barely come
To find the forces that he may command,
That his dear day completes its largest sum
Within the darkness creeping o'er the land?
Why should the warning come so soon, so soon,
That all his bravest work must change and pass,
And but the margin of the afternoon
May be reflected from his finest glass?
The spirit falters 'neath the sinking sun,
But whoso reads himself and God aright
Must know that even when the day is done
He still may grasp new measures of delight, —
  That all his strength may haply be more strong
  As moved upon by some great even-song.

II

How sweet the shadows are that softly close
Upon the shifting boundaries of the world
Against the gonfalons of gold and rose
Through all the sky so wondrously unfurled!
How fair and free the countless banners float,
Borne onward in their royal pageantry,
Till every hill and plain, howe'er remote,
Thrills back the sense of some new harmony!
And when the glory fades amid the hush
That deepens downward with the deepening mist,
The dreams of men take on the morning flush
That shimmers through the evening amethyst.
  Only the blessèd child may enter in
  The kingdoms where the heavenly powers begin.

III

"What matter if the earth grow less and less,"
My heart repeated in a glad refrain,
"When such a revelation can express
The fulness of such far exceeding gain?"
All I had ever known or felt before
Of truth or fealty or transcendent toil,
Appeared to me a new-created store
Upspringing from a new-created soil;
Yet all I was and all I yet might be
Was holden by the world's unbroken claim,
I could not draw the breath of liberty
Save in the service it should chance to frame.—
  With every fiber of the soul's increase
  Some new demand requires the touch of peace.

IV

I felt myself encompassed by a cloud
Of shining witnesses for love and truth,
In life-long mysteries that breathed aloud
The blessed surety of eternal youth.
The tender tones that tremble o'er the line
Where silence waits upon the shores of sound
Filled all my thought with music so divine
Utmost desire no further could abound.
And with my sacred joy I marveled much
That any human heart had ever heard
The dull half-notes that my imperfect touch
Had ventured forth as my expressive word, —
  So small my labor seemed, so large the sphere
  Where heaven and earth as blent in one appear.

V

O loyal Love, whatever may betide
The simple song that means so much to me,
What guerdon may be given or denied,
Still every chord is true as truth to thee;
It still responds to that great over-love
Which from the first has prompted all my quest,
And, knowing this, how should we care to prove
By praise or blame what may be worst or best?
Yet with the sweet assurance and content
That good work brings throughout the busy day,
I could but feel the forces still unspent,
And press more earnestly upon my way.
  But with the very most my love could do,
  To thee, O Love, it still were only true.

VI

I well remember once when we had read
How every spoken word that men might share
Can never be as lost or void or dead,
But lives forever in the moving air, —
How long we questioned if the careless tones
That we sent forth should circle round again,
And if we should escape the playful moans
We mingled with the speech we uttered then.
But now the echoes whispering far and near
Brought back so much of my poor melody,
Through every change I could not help but hear
The lingering burden of its varied key, —
  And then I knew that no one might evade
  The slightest wingèd note he had betrayed.

VII

Thanks be to God whose all-sufficient grace
Inspires the faint beginning with the end:
His mercy does not ask us to replace
The broken chords no human power can mend;
But note by note he leads us surely on,
And fashions all our effort to the plan
Whereby the summits of eternal dawn
Are lifted over every bar and ban.
And so I sung the wider, freer hope
That stretched away before my raptured sight,—
Sung all I fathomed in the boundless scope
That lay beyond the borders of the night;
  For I had found, with naught to intervene,
  The mighty rhythm of the vast serene.

THE PERFECT LIGHT

I

As day to day proclaims its tender speech,
And night to night its knowledge doth declare,
The gift of life can never fail to reach
The kindred life created otherwhere.
The living word speeds onward to its own,
Nor stops for any guerdon or reply,
Content to feel in every slightest tone
The beauty and delight that never die.
And so the singer who restored in song
The sacred symbol of the heavenly fire,
And those who come its marvels to prolong,
Are linked forever in the one desire;
  For God and man and music yet to be
  Have wrought upon their inmost harmony.

II

Who seeks the source of song must look to Him
In whom all rhythm and response are made, —
From drifting dust to chanting cherubim
Who sight his face serene and unafraid;
The One who was before the worlds could swing
In their completion round the central sun
Inspired the touch that countless eons bring
To frame the inspiration just begun;
And through the ages every quickening strain
That echoes through the rarest works of men
Has found the self-same glory to attain,
Repeated over ever and again:
  All that is good or true in any wise
  Only through Him receives its radiant guise.

III

I wonder who in some transcendent time
Shall read the story of our wondrous race,
And measure forth the full prolific rhyme
That waits upon the truth we cannot trace.
We only glimpse the bright, unbroken thread
That reaches from the first resultant power
Through all the forces that have surely led
Into the largess of the passing hour;
But when the sense of some surpassing seer
Awakens in the world's supreme advance,
Then all the splendid purpose shall appear
That overrules the meanest circumstance,
  And men shall fathom out the blessed way
  That treasures up its gold in such poor clay.

IV

Whatever beauty this dear life may see
In full expression of divine intent,
From first to last its matchless poetry
Reflects the Christ in every element.
What precious art found fruitage in the earth
Before the dayspring touched the weary sky,
Its ministry was guided in the worth
The Son of God illumined from on high.
And since he drained the sacrificial cup,
Utmost humanity at last complete,
Whatever loveliness is lifted up
Bears out the mission of the Paraclete.
  The comfort and the joy and deep acclaim
  Attest the spirit of the cloven flame.

V

O thou Great Love wherein all other love
Must find the secret of its farthest sphere,
The least adventure were enough to prove
The need of love too great for any fear.
And thy majestic work in shaping out
Such royal profit for the heart of man
Fulfills the freedom that is borne about
The endless growth of his appointed plan.
Thy tender touch hath set no metes or bounds
Save its own law in any soul or sense, —
No limit holds the promise that surrounds
The imagery of thy omnipotence;
  And love begetting love, it shall define
  From step to step its uttermost design.

VI

Some things there be upon this sounding shore
Where music makes such endless mysteries
That have no measure in our deepest lore
For any phase of their glad harmonies.
But faith and feeling through the sacred tide
Have no despair or danger of eclipse,
Though every word may haply be denied
That might affirm the great apocalypse;
And when the happy hope has passed the bar
That holds it here from its supernal joy,
No melody can be too fine or far
For its unfettered forces to employ;
  The vision and the voice shall then essay
  All that the earthly form could not convey.

VII

The end of song and its supreme delight,
The end of life and its remotest art,
Are given forth when life and song unite
In keeping with the heavenly counterpart.
When human love completes the shining round
That love's divinity has breathed upon,
And through the white effulgence God is found
Blending the beauty of celestial dawn;
Then life and love together shall behold,
As born anew within their vast estate,
Their larger labor fitted to the mould
That most exalted effort shall create, —
  And more and more the singer shall abide
  Whom love and life have wholly satisfied.

www.ingramcontent.com/pod-product-compliance
Lightning Source LLC
Chambersburg PA
CBHW031400160426
43196CB00007B/832